Is That You Boy!

by

Noel Magnier

1st Edition December 2000
Reprint 2005 Cork City European Capital of Culture

Dedication

In memory of my parents John and Priscilla
and my brother Billy,
who was lost at sea May 7th, 1964.
May they rest in peace

In memory of my brother Bill lost overboard from the
M.V. Irish plane off Key West, Florida,
on May 7th 1964. Age 24 yrs.

Bill

(1940 - 1964)

What do you do when you lose your son
and you know that you're hell on earth has begun
You go and creep into a shell of your own,
where no one can touch you or reach you to mourn,
and you know you are wrong,
as there are others there too
Dad, sisters and brothers who loved him like you.
But grief is so selfish and hard to be shared,
when you think of the tough little boy that you reared.
His little face dirty when you'd only just scrubbed him
and the fudgies he'd keep in this pocket were something
a magnet, old buttons, some nails, rusty screws, old comics, ball
bearings he'd swap them for sure!
Then a few little years and the sea raised her finger
She was born in his blood, not long did he linger
His fate was in her hands so what could we do
As she gently closed oer him her mantle of blue

by his Mam Prissie

Contents

Acknowledgments

I would like to thank the following for their help and support

The Irish Examiner for allowing me
reproduce photographs from their files.

Shay Curtin of Quality Print, Sheares
Street, Cork for his permission to repro-
duce photographs from his Old Cork
Collection.

My dear friend Richard T. Cooke for his
faith and his inspiration.

Mary D. O'Connor of Typing Times,
Ballincollig, Co. Cork for typesetting,
designing the book.

Richard Lynch of Rainbow Print,
Barrack Street, Cork for his help.

My wife Jenny and our family for
putting up with me during the writing of
this book.

My daughter Jacqueline in Boston, USA.

Introduction

Is That You Boy! recounts the exploits of one particular gang, their scams and schemes to make much needed pocket money in the Cork of the 1940s and '50s.

A sort of 'Bowery Boys' operation where headquarters was not Louies Ice-cream Parlour (The Bronx) but Julia's Milk and Cafe Shop at the top of Shandon street where the 'scams' were hatched and the measure of a gang member was judged by the number of pints of milk he could consume at a single session and where new gang members were initiated by drinking a pint of thick sour milk brought in from Gills Emporium next door to Julias.

> *"He who lives by the baa*
> *may die by the baa"*
>
> **Foley.**

Chapter 1

Kids Of Today Have It All

The kids of today have it all … computers, videos, satellite and digital TV also laser, quasar, swimming pools, huge stadiums, hydro gyms, the list goes on and still they (the kids) say they are bored. Do the kids of today ever wonder how their Mothers and Fathers (and Grandparents) enjoyed themselves in their day and survive to tell the tale? Earning money in those days of the 40's and 50's was not easy, yet we came up with some great ideas to keep ourselves in pocket money. Things like going for blocks and turf for the old people with the boxcar. Then to Denny's Cellar on the Watercourse Road for the 'Pickle' which was brought in the family bath to the various shops that sold meat. Spending summers in Denny's Cellar cleaning out the pig lorries and getting a few lops from the owner and sometimes we would get two shillings or even a half crown if the lorry was a double decker. One time I got a ten bob (ten shilling) note from Mr. Murphy because he said the price of pigs was "Grand" and sure didn't he dance one time with my mother down in The Arcadia. He said she was a beautiful lady, and of course I agreed.

We were never short of ways to spend our money and The Pictures were always top of the list and what a choice we had, The Savoy, The Pavilion, The Palace, The Coliseum, The Lee, The Ritz, The Assembly Rooms, Miahas, Saint Mary's Hall, The Lido (and I still probably left out one or two more). We would also buy huge ice-creams which we got from The Polar Ice Cream Company in The South Mall. They were so big they could last you almost the entire day. Then we would take the bus down to the very end of Blackrock. We would get off and go to this shop where there was a beautiful parrot with a terrible tongue. We used to call it 'The Cursing Parrot' and tease it to use bad language. We often spent hours in the shop drinking lemonade and eating cakes and most especially teaching that parrot new curses that we brought down from the city. Later, broke again, we would always keep just the bare amount for the bus home.

There were many more schemes and scams to make money (and indeed to spend it) all will be revealed as you meander through this book.

Talking about 'Tales of the Unexpected' well you ain't heard nothin' till you have finished every morsel and one can only hope that once you have digested everything you may pay heed to the immortal words - Don't try this at home!

* * *

Chapter 2

The Toblerone Affair

Larry was the leader of our gang and he knew how to make the most of his status as 'kingpin' of the lane. Larry would never call for anybody to their house, it was always somebody calling to his house, he was the boss, 'The Main Man'. So, if you wanted Larry you would tap at the window and ask, "is Larry there please?"
"He'll be out now, boy", would come the reply from inside. It was usually his sister who would answer.

You had to wait outside for Larry, come rain or shine, few, if any, were let in, that was the way it was, nobody asked any questions. Larry would come out when he was ready. It could be anything up to an hour and you never knocked twice either. Larry wielded a lot of power and he enjoyed it. To be part of his gang was a privilege and indeed one paid for that privilege. Tommy paid Larry a three penny piece every week, Friday was pay-day, and on the 'button' every Friday, he was paid. Tommy could afford the three pence because his father was a plasterer. Michael used to pay Larry by bringing him to his house to play, once every week. Michael was an only child, unusual in those days, he had a fantastic collection of toy soldiers, cowboys and Indians, aeroplanes, tanks. To be asked to stay for tea was a rare privilege bestowed only on the few - Larry was one of the few. Michael wanted to be in Larry's gang, and Michael's parents were happy to go along with this.

Other members of the gang would make regular contributions by way of American comics or cigarette cards. Larry was partial to chocolate, but, there was one particular bar that eluded Larry, as it did the rest of the gang, that was the 'king' of all chocolate bars - the mighty Toblerone. Now there was grandeur for you! To have possession of a Toblerone, the Rolls Royce of chocolate bars, was an ambition few could hope to achieve when the average pocket money was only a penny a week, if you were lucky!

Now one could save up for a 'Toblerone' and indeed a few tried, for the first few weeks at least, but other emergencies cropped up and the savings were quickly used. This time Larry was determined to succeed and he increased the 'membership' fee on Tommy and requested more American

A birthday party down Bulldog (Hillgrove) Lane in the 1920s.
My mother, Priscilla 3rd from left.

comics which he would sell in school to raise the required finance.

This particular day Larry called us together and announced he had enough money to put a deposit on the Toblerone and we were ordered to march up to Liz Ann's shop, which was half way up Gerald Griffin Street on the left hand side. There in the shop window, standing out majestically from the rest of the goodies was the source of Larry's ambition, the Toblerone.

Liz Ann was surprised to see the gang of six arrive, we took up the entire shop. Poor Liz Ann, not used to such a crowd, anticipated a bonanza, alas however, Larry was the only one with money and he handed over the deposit promising that he would be back the following Friday to claim his prize. True to his promise Larry, along with the rest of us, arrived at the shop and with admiration, tinged with envy we stood in awe as Larry, on handing over the balance of the money to Liz Ann was handed the bar of Toblerone. Larry had done it!

We left the shop with Larry, the Toblerone held high in his hand as we galloped down the street on our imaginary horses to the safety of the 'lane' and stopped breathless outside Larry's house. He went inside to show his family the prized bar and kept us waiting for a good half hour before he emerged. He told us he was going to have a draw the following day, Saturday, for a piece of the Toblerone. We were to gather at eleven o'clock in the morning sharp and with that Larry went indoors only to appear at the window 'flashing' the Toblerone at us. We dispersed, drooling at the prospect of being the lucky winner. Saturday could not come soon enough.

That morning to a man we were outside Larry's door at

eleven o'clock sharp. We could see the Toblerone on display in Larry's window. It was untouched, nobody had been given a bit yet. Larry, true to form, emerged almost an hour later and declared the draw would be a number between one and ten thousand. We could not believe our ears but on we went guessing.

"39?"

"No."

"870?"

"No."

"5,555?"

"No."

"7,543?" said Tommy in exasperation.

"No" said Larry, "but ye're getting warm". So on we went, until Larry had to go in home to the toilet.

That was to be his big mistake for we decided we had enough of him and his Toblerone, we agreed to 'jump' him when he came out. We didn't give him a chance. We were on him in an instant and using his braces we tied his hands and feet together, grabbed the Toblerone from him and we took off up the lane for Patrick's Arch where we stopped to divide the spoils. In a matter of seconds, Larry's Toblerone was devoured.

We agreed he had pushed us too far on this one, imagine a draw for a piece of chocolate, "One to ten thousand!" Some hope of getting that, the bloody thing would melt before any of us would guess that. Anyway, the laugh was on Larry, and he would have to start saving all over again if he wanted to have another Toblerone.

* * *

Chapter 3

The Point Of Extraction
The Tooth, The Whole Tooth
And Nothing But The Tooth

When a certain dentist pulled a good tooth instead of a 'bad' one belonging to my sister, necessitating another trip back to have the bad one removed at two bob a tooth it was time to call halt, this was the second time a member of our family had the wrong tooth extracted. Others in our street had similar experiences with the same dentist and he became known as the 'Liar-y Dentist' (because he could never tell the 'tooth'). Others called him 'Double Extractions'. Something had to be done to replace 'The Liar-y Dentist' and quick, because a toothache was a terrible thing to endure and teeth that were bad just had to go.

A conference was called, the three brothers Billy, Pat and myself. The topic – pulling teeth and how to make it pay. After some discussion a plan was agreed, but, would it work? An experiment was needed. Pat was the one who drew the 'short' match, he was the Guinea Pig. I was to be the 'dentist' and Bill my assistant. Poor Pat, was to be our first patient. He had not a bad tooth in his head but we soon 'fixed' that by selecting a tooth at the back of his mouth. We took turns at loosening the tooth by pushing it to and fro until it became loose and ready for 'extraction'.

The method of extraction was agreed. The tooth was about to be removed, our parents would have no idea what we were at, it was Saturday morning and mother was gone shopping, father to the bookies to back a few horses the two sisters gone to play with their pals the coast was clear. The moment had arrived, Bill had the twine, it was well tested for its strength and was about two feet long. A loop was made at one end and the other end was put through this loop and deftly placed around the 'offending ' tooth, when the twine was tightened around the tooth, "the patient" was directed to sit on the other side of the door. It was my job to attach the twine to the door handle. Bill, on the other side of the door, was awaiting my instructions. Pat, who had been very brave until now, was getting distinctly nervous (and who could blame him), but the thought of the price of the Lido was his inspiration. Bill was ready outside, we were ready inside.

"Ready Bill", said I.
"Ready when you are", came Bill's reply.
"O.K. Bill", said I, "on the count of three pull as fast as you can".
"O.K., Ready, One, Two, Three p-u-l-l."

Bill was strong and could pull like a bullet out shot the tooth. Pat howled with fright and pain, but only for a mere thirty seconds for the 'extraction' was so neat that the three of us fell around the place laughing and the prospect of our first, er - 'patient'.

We had not long to wait, about two hours later Bill arrived with our first customer, Teddy Cummins, from the street was 'murdered' from the pain in his tooth it was Saturday, the "Liar-y Dentist" was closed, as he had two shillings given him by his father, Teddy was assured of 'first class treatment'. It was a fair sized molar and though somewhat decayed it was on closer examination very sturdy and needed some preliminary loosening. So when Teddy's tooth was ready for extraction he was howling with pain, but was assured that in two minutes his agony would be over as we were ready for the main work. Teddy was given a 'mouthwash' of lukewarm water and told to rinse his mouth (just as if he were at the 'real' dentist).

Pat had the twine tied to the doorknob, Bill was ready on the other side of the door, I placed the twine around Teddy's tooth his eyes were closed tightly as he trembled at the thought of further pain to come.

"O.K. Pat", said I, "ready?" and to Bill, "stand by".
"I'm ready", said Bill.
Pat, had Teddy's arms pinned so as to take the pressure when Bill would pull the door.
"Right" said I, "on the count of three, one – two – three , p-u-l-l".

Bill pulled, Teddy cried out in agony. This time he was screaming at the top of his voice with tears flowing down his face. Then he realised it was all over, opened his eyes slowly and through the tears could see Pat dangling the cause of his trouble. The offending molar was well and truly removed, never again to cause Teddy any bother. A quick mouthwash, some cotton wool into the gaping socket - a now smiling Teddy gratefully handed over his two shilling piece, promising to spread the word about our 'efficient practice'.

Just as Teddy was leaving, the door opened and in came Mother from her shopping trip to town. Her expression of relief at being home quickly changed to anger as she took in the scene that greeted her. Teddy Cummins had his hanky to his mouth and it covered in blood. There were pieces of bloodied cotton wool on the table and on the floor.

"What in the name of God is going on here?" she said. "That boy looks terrible, where did all that blood come from?". You, You" said mother, looking at me ."You better tell me what exactly is going on in my house. Now!"

"We're just playing, Mother" said I, "playing dentist, and Teddy had a bad tooth and he was screaming and roaring from the pain in it and we pulled it out for him and now he's grand and the tooth and the terrible pain are gone".

As the truth dawned on Mother she cooled down somewhat, but not before I got a clip on the ear and was ordered, "never again to dream of pulling someone's teeth", and give that boy his money back, she would go straight away to his parents and explain what happened.

The hardest part for me was giving Teddy Cummins his two shillings back. Bill and Pat at this stage had done 'a runner', bolting out the back door to 'escape Mother's wrath' as my budding career in dentistry lay in tatters.

* * *

Chapter 4

The Flo Mulligan Affair

Christmas time in the 1950's was always eagerly looked forward to. Early November the first signs would appear when Noonan's Shop in Gerald Griffin Street would remove their stock of hardware from their big window and start filling it with fantastic toys and magical Christmas lights that blinked on and off. From the bedroom window of our house which was just across the street, the three of us watched mesmerised as Monny Noonan 'dressed' the window.

We waited with bathed breath for the first sign of a cowboy hat to appear then the gleaming silver guns and rifles and the Indian outfits with the big feather headband and moccasin waistcoat and of course the knife.

Visions of 'Tonto' and 'The Lone Ranger' loomed before us as we gazed in awe at Noonans window. Then the harsh reality of our predicament, how could we get our hands on all that wonderful stuff? We knew Mother paid a few pence into the Christmas Club every week and sure God help her there was three of us to buy for. She didn't know we knew she was paying into this Christmas Club. She thought her three little darlings still believed in Santa Claus ... and we

did too, when it suited us. We knew things were not easy for
Mother. What with the Father away in France, fighting the
war. A Corporal in The Pioneer Corps with the British Army.
(We all laughed a lot about Da being in the 'Pioneer Corps'
of all things and he fond of the pint!)
We needed a plan if we were to afford what they had in
Noonan's window and it had to be a good one. We called a
meeting of the 'Gang' to ask for suggestions. Some ideas
would have put us away in a Reformatory for years - robbing
the penny bank in Saint Mary's Hall, or Longys idea, to rob
old Maggie Duggans boxcar full of apples and sell them
outside The Lido. Flynny's idea to buy a bonham and rare it
to be a big pig and sell it on was an idea for another time.
'Blackie White' made the supreme suggestion …
"Lads", said Blackie, "Ye can have my granda's war medals
if ye're really stuck. He keeps them in a shoe box under the
bed and we would get good money for them in Jones Pawn
in Shandon Street."

We thanked Blackie for his fine gesture and gave him a
solemn promise that in the not too distant future his granda's
medals would once again be called into active service. Then I
unfolded the master plan. "Gentlemen", I said, in the most
impressive voice I could muster, "We are about to go into the
kidnapping Dognapping Business". The lads huddled closer
to hear the game plan. This was it, down our street lived the
Mulligans, an elderly couple with no family, their pride and
joy was their little Yorkshire Terrier, Flo, known to all in the
street as Flo Mulligan. Flo was the target. There would be
big money in this we agreed. The Mulligans were probably
the richest people in the street. "Lads if we pull this one off -
and we will, believe me we will be able to buy anything in
Monny Noonan's window. How do ye' all feel about," I said.
There was a chorus of "Yes - Yes - Yes" as we all touched
wrists - like Red Indians we were Blood Brothers.

Everything was planned to perfection - we knew not many people came into Mulligans' Shop as they kept very few sweets and things and Flo was always jumping up and down on the counter and sometimes in the window. We chose a Friday evening in early December, it was dark with rain falling as we moved into action. There were few people around which suited us perfectly, the gas lights in the street seemed to be dimmer than usual. Every one of us knew what we had to do, God how many times did we rehearse it? We were as ready as we could be. Flynny was the keyman and he had 'Josser' his little terrier ready to tempt Flo. Foley and Longy were eager with anticipation. From my position in Peacock Lane I had a clear view of Mulligans, Billy and Pat were close by with an old L.D.F (Local Defence Force) overcoat which the mother got from Billy Lane (for the bed if the weather got too cold). The coat was huge, it was in case Longy missed Flo with his jumper. We thought of

Neighbours from Farren Street, Bull Dog Lane, Patrick's Arch, Peacock Lane, Chapel Lane and Gerald Griffin Street on an outing in the 1960s.

everything. "Right boys, the coast is clear. Go for it …
Now!" Flynny's timing was perfection, into the shop he went
with 'Josser' who gave a little yelp, Flo was on the counter
like a flash. Flynny moved for the door, Foley held the door
open and like a shot Longy dived on Flo, wrapped the dog in
the jumper, they made a beeline for Peacock Lane and
Longys house. It only took a few seconds. Mr. and Mrs.
Mulligan, in a state of shock, ran on to the street frantically
shouting, "Flo, Flo, Here Flo, Here Flo", but of course there
was no sign of Flo. The word soon spread that Flo was
missing and that the Mulligans were offering a five pound
note for Flo's safe return. "God Almighty, a fiver, a whole
bloody fiver!" said Flynny. The following morning we met in
Longys brother's pigeon loft. The brother had sold all the
pigeons so the loft was a perfect place to keep Flo. In the
meantime the guards were called in, that worried me as I had
to tell the Mulligans that I had found their precious 'Flo'. I
needn't have worried though for when I walked into
Mulligans shop that Saturday afternoon with the dog safe and
sound in my arms, Mrs. Mulligan with tears rolling down her
face kissed and hugged Flo so much that she hardly knew I
existed.

"Where in God's name did you find Flo," said an obviously
relieved Mr. Mulligan as he pressed a crispy English five
pound note into my hand. "I found her down in Pouraddy
Harbour Mr. Mulligan", said I as I stood there staring in awe
at this strange looking five pound note and wondering how in
the name of God would you split five pounds between six of
us? Well sure that was another days work.

* * *

Chapter 5

Flag Days

Flag days were a 'God send' and the good Nuns were delighted when the three darling brothers volunteered their 'services' for their latest charity.

The day for selling was Saturday (there was no school). We couldn't wait for Saturday to come. Up with the lark, we were down to the Convent for eight thirty. Sister Teresa was giving out the boxes. One box per person and a little bag of flags. Each box was numbered so Sister would record the person's name on a list opposite the number. She would tell us how wonderful we are and the 'little flower' would grant us any favour we wanted for being such good little boys and "by the way", she said, "each boy will get a spearmint bar and an apple when they come back at five o'clock with the boxes, and all the flags sold. So off with you now and don't forget to stop and say the Angelus at twelve o'clock".

The three of us took off. Pat was going to Patrick's Bridge on my instructions Bill was given the Blackpool territory, I would take up place on the North Gate Bridge, a most strategic position. I had the main artery to town covered because most people came from the Northside to town and they had to cross the bridge and me.

As usual we put a miraculous medal into the box to give it a rattle, as we shook it in someone's face it would sound as if some flags had already been bought, it gave us what we called 'a start'.

From ten o'clock the people would begin to appear, first a trickle ... by eleven o'clock a steady flow would be the norm. "Mrs. buy a flag for the little flowers altar" in fairness the response was always brilliant. The people were charitable. Pennies and three penny bits were the usual contributions, sometime you would get a tanner (a six penny bit). Occasionally a person put a shilling in the box, others would put two bob or a half crown in. One time a priest put a pound note into my box, I had to remove it for safety.

By two o'clock the box was getting heavy, things were going well. I was wondering how Bill and Pat were doing?

If they were doing as well as me we were in for a clean up. We had arranged to meet at four o'clock behind St. Mary's Hall Picture House (opposite the North Chapel). I got there ten minutes to four, my box full to the brim and every flag sold. Sister Teresa would be delighted, however she would be far from pleased if she knew what was to happen next, while I was waiting for the boys with their boxes I decided to work on mine having borrowed a long kitchen knife from home I got down to business. The idea being to slide the knife in the opening of the box, the tricky bit, to slide money on to the blade and trying to tease it out through the narrow opening. This took a fair bit of skill for if the opening was damaged in any way some awkward questions would be asked. Six penny pieces (especially the English ones) were grand and slim and if you saw the slightest glimpse of a shilling appearing at the opening there was a feeling of great excitement. A steady hand was required, the slightest wrong move would dislodge it and it could be lost never again to be found.

I had removed my share by the time the boys arrived 'bang on' four o'clock. We agreed that the limit was ten bob each, if we had full boxes and all the flags sold. We all had full boxes. As I was regarded as the 'expert' at removing the money it did not take long to take 'our wages' as we called it from the boxes, in a matter of minutes the operation was complete. Ten bob each was a small fortune for us, we would give mother half and we would still have a sizeable five bob a 'man' each. It was time to go and return the boxes, we agreed we would go one by one at five minute intervals to the Convent. Sister Teresa was delighted and with good reason. When she took the boxes in her hands a broad smile crossed her face.

"Well done boys", she said, "ye had a great day. The Little Flower will be very pleased", and she handed each of us a spearmint bar and an apple. "Thank you very much sister," said each of us dutifully, as we received our 'reward'.

"Let us know when you want us again, we love spearmint and apples". "See you next flag day, Sister".

* * *

Chapter 6

Slot Machines
- A Regular Check Up

S lot machines were a constant source of fascination to us kids, we were always working on systems to crack them. We felt there had to be a formula which would make us rich.

The slot machines were our main interest when the 'Merrys' came to the Mardyke, we also had an interest in the horse racing which we knew was only pure luck. The little man in charge would sell tickets with the names of jockeys for a penny each, when his quota was sold he'd press a switch and shout, "And their off!" the lights with the jockeys name would flash on and off a screen in an imaginary race for about a minute until it came to a stop with just one name lighting the screen and then the small man would cry out, "And the winner is … 'Beasley'". 'Dines' was another name that seemed to win often but it was the slot machines that we were after. If you cracked them you were made.

The 'checks' paid good money - 15 pennys was the big

payout on the 'White' there was one white on the dial. The Two yellows which paid out eight pennys and four greens paid four pennys. There were many blacks and reds which paid only tuppence (two). We would never touch a 'cold' slot machine in the 'Merrys'. We would stand and watch others play. When one player got broke we would move in on that machine. The first thing we did was give it a hefty couple of blows on the side to see if there was any money stuck in the pay-out chute. That treatment often paid rich dividends. If the person in charge caught you, you would be escorted out of the grounds getting a kick in the backside from a steel-toed boot. In a never ending search for the formula we devised various codes, such as counting how far the 'White' was away from the payout chute, if it was seven colours

Teacher, Lizzie Healy, and her pupils in the North Presentation 'Machine Room' in Chapel Lane, now Cathedral Walk where they manufactured stockings for the altar boys of Cork in the early 1930s.

adrift we would put in the penny, pull the handle and wait for the big payout which rarely if ever came. Another system was to stall the handle that is to pull the handle gently and move the numbers to a point in the dial where the 'White' was poised over the payout chute, then quickly pull the handle all the way. Unfortunately, this didn't work too often either. It was hard to crack the checks at the Merrys.

We had more luck with Shop Checks, one in particular was a goldmine. Situated in a shop on Dominic Street near Shandon. One day when playing it I discovered there was no back to the machine. Apparently the owner removed it because he took pennys for change on a regular basis and always put the equivalent in silver into the back of the machine. This was an incredible find. Just slip a few fingers round the back and a search would reveal the treasure-trove, a two shilling piece, a half crown, three or maybe four single shillings. It was like we had discovered Aladdin's Cave but as the saying goes, "All good things must come to an end", we had paid one trip too many to this particular 'Cave'. The shop owner and his son had finally copped on that we were the culprits (we were to learn later that the shop owner was blaming his son for the missing silver). They closed the shop door with the three of us inside then made us empty our pockets. They kept what money we had and warned us never to come in to their shop again. Then they opened the door to let us out and we ran like hell up Dominic Street with the shouts and threats of the shopkeeper and his son ringing in our ears.

* * *

Chapter 7

The Great Picture Show

As usual a supply of ready cash was a constant challenge to one's entrepreneurial expertise. We had often discussed putting on our own Picture Show.

We put the word out that the pictures would be held in our house on Saturday afternoon and admission prices were a penny for the ten to twelve year olds, a half penny for the seven to eight year olds and a farthing for the four to five year olds. A big crowd was expected. Timing was to be very important, especially staying out of the way of disgruntled parents, for the truth of the matter was that we knew what we were about to do was something different to the Picture Show.

As Saturday drew closer our plan was taking shape, we had decided we would show a religious film, to stay on the right side of parents who could hardly refuse the kids money to see the 'Stations of the Cross'.

The material for the show were religious leaflets which we were given every month in school, we had to keep them in our prayer book so a considerable collection was available. The idea for the film was that leaflets which depicted the various Stations of the Cross would be selected in proper sequence and pasted to the wall in what we called the 'Back Passage' of our house.

 The 'Back Passage' was strategically situated between the entrance from the street and the exit through to the sizeable back yard which had an exit out to the lane. Just perfect.

Saturday was upon us, the word had got around and there was a queue forming from 2.00pm with the show starting at 3.00. We were ready for them. Billy was put on the door for crowd control, he was burly and tough and he would take the money. There would be no messing with Billy around.

Unlike the Picture House we would allow three kids in at the time to 'enjoy' the film, the 'Stations of the Cross'. As the projectionist my most important piece of equipment was the flashlamp I got last Christmas.

So it was ready, steady go! for the great Picture Show. The first customer was called to the 'screen' I turned the light on the first leaflet which showed 'The Agony in the Garden' then next to 'Jesus before Pontius Pilate' me explaining what it was all about and mimicking the voices of the various central figures in this unfolding biblical epic. Then quickly to 'Jesus falls the third time', more quickly to 'The Crucifixion' and happily to 'The Resurrection'. A happy ending was, we agreed, important. Then the bemused customer was ushered by Pat out to the back yard and passed on to Bridie.

We could not allow anyone to leave the back yard until everyone had seen the film, and in no time at all twenty customers had seen the show and were out in the back yard

The family home at 27 Gerard Griffin Street, with sisters May and Christina Allen (Author's Grandaunt and Grandmother) standing at the front door. *Note: Unknown person at upstairs window also the gable which shows the entrance to Bulldog Lane.*

awaiting their release. With a few kids remaining to see the show the battery of the flashlamp began to dim and not having a spare, urgent action was needed. Salt was applied to the battery and it was then placed on the range in the kitchen to be heated. This operation had to be repeated a few times until all had seen the film. Then the crowd of mainly dissatisfied customers were released 'en masse' from the security of the back yard. Bridie had done a great job and the free raffle for a three penny bit seemed to have done the trick in ensuring that no riot took place.

After the show we divided the profits and took off to the real pictures, The Lido.

Moriarty's Lane, a typical Cork laneway of the era.
(Courtesy Irish Examiner)

Chapter 8

The Donkey And The Sawdust

It would be very difficult for young people in today's world to realise how important sawdust was as an everyday commodity. The main users of sawdust were butchers, public houses and barber shops. They would spread the sawdust on stone or timber floors - there was little by way of carpet or linoleum in those days.

Two timber yards in our immediate area supplied the sawdust. The timber yard in Burke's Avenue (or Johnson's Lane as it was better known) was our first choice for sawdust because Mr. Harris (who lost an arm in an accident in the timberyard) would always give you a good big bag for sixpence. The other was O'Shea's on the Watercourse Road. Another great user of sawdust was the many piggeries in the area. The pigs were comfortable when they had a bed of sawdust and pig owners bought a lot of it. One of the bigger suppliers had their place beside the piggeries. Two brothers ran the operation and this is where the story really begins about the donkey and the sawdust.

As big sawdust suppliers, the brothers could be seen going regularly to the timber yards on their donkey and cart and coming back loaded with bags of the precious stuff. We knew where they would store the bags prior to sale and a decision was made to - er -'borrow' a few bags for sale to our neighbours who had sawdust fires. We knew from observing their route that the brothers went shopping together every Thursday evening at about - 5.00pm. We hatched our plan for this particular Thursday evening - the plan, to load the donkey and cart with as many bags of sawdust as possible and hide them in a shed in our backyard. So, on this cold, dark November evening, Bill and myself (Pat would not come as he was afraid that this was too dangerous) made our way to the yard where the sawdust was stored in a dry shed along with the donkey and cart.

Old Cattle Market, from where we 'borrowed' the donkey and the sawdust. *(Courtesy Irish Examiner)*

Getting into the yard was no problem, a few seconds more and we were inside the shed. Luckily for us the donkey never brayed and in thanks we gave the ass a few bales of hay from the stock as a reward to chew on whilst we loaded the cart with bags of sawdust, then we had to hitch the cart to the donkey and though we had the tackle and reins we had not a clue how to harness the donkey to the cart as time was running out we decided to abandon the cart. Instead, we loaded four bags of sawdust on the donkey's back and tied them with ropes we found in the shed. Off we went with only four instead of eight bags, still it was better than nothing. We headed off in the dark to our destination which was only about fifteen minutes away, home. There was Billy, pulling the poor donkey by the reins, I was holding on to the bags to prevent them sliding off the donkey's back. This was a difficult task as every movement of the donkey dislodged the cargo, I was holding on to them for dear life. We got to our destination, Bulldog Lane, by the side of our house, we had left the side gate unbolted and quickly off-loaded the bags from the donkey and hid the sawdust in the shed in our back yard under a load of old clothes which we were keeping for the rag and bone man.

Then we brought the donkey to the top of the lane faced him for the North Chapel gave him a quick slap on the rump, the donkey took off with such relief that the poor animal did an almighty pee before taking off like a racehorse. We knew the donkey would be 'home' in no time. Billy and myself fell around the place laughing and congratulating ourselves on our success as we dusted the sawdust from our clothes and shoes and went in home where Mother expressed surprise at seeing her little darlings in this early. We went to bed and talked about the rewards that would be coming our way from the sale of 'the golden sawdust' we fell asleep dreaming of the huge ice creams we would buy and the money we would have for pitch and toss.

The following morning we were awakened by the sound of mother screaming at us and pulling the bed clothes off.

"Get out of that bed, the two of ye", she roared. "Get your clothes and get down that stairs". She lashed into the two of us with a walking cane she had bought in Statia Cahills shop by the North Chapel.

As the two of us ran, almost fell, down the stairs with mother and the 'walking cane' in hot pursuit we were stopped in our tracks by the presence of Garda Downey from Watercourse Road and another man we instantly recognised through our pain (Mother was still lashing us). When she stopped Guard Downey asked us,

"Tell me what did you do with the sawdust ye stole from this man?", pointing towards the man who didn't open his mouth. Bill looked at me and I looked at him and we both knew the game was up, we told the Garda the sawdust was in the shed down the yard.

"How in God's name", said mother to the Garda, "did ye find that it was my two brats who stole this man's sawdust?". This time the man piped up "Mrs.", he said "'twas very easy, there were holes in the bags of sawdust and all I had to do was to follow the trail of sawdust on the ground and it stopped at your back gate. It was as simple as that Mrs. So if I can have the bags of sawdust I will ask the Garda to forget all about it as I can see you are well able to dish out your own justice, and by the way", said the man turning to myself and Billy, "lucky for the two of ye the donkey came home safely".

The man took off with his bags of sawdust, the Garda left us with a severe warning that there better not be a next time, Mother gave us a few more lashes of the cane and sent us to school without breakfast whilst brother Pat sat at the table, angelic-like, eating an extra portion of porridge for being such a good boy and for having nothing to do with the two of 'them' who have only "sawdust where their brains should be".

* * *

Chapter 9

Fag Boxes - Worth A Fortune

but beware of the baa

When money was in short supply (and that was most times) in order to keep our hand in we needed to improvise, and we did with empty fag boxes. There was a few popular brands which were always in demand 'Woodbines', the proper name for this most popular of cigarettes was 'Wills Wild Woodbines', known to us as 'The Three Ws'. We would go in to shops and ask the person inside the counter, "Have you any Wild Woodbines please?" If the reply was "Yes" we would say as we ran out of the premises, "Would you ever tame them," and we would fall around the place laughing our sides off. Yet the woodbine packet became a symbol of currency along with other brands such as 'Gold Flake', 'Kerry Blues', 'Capstan' and 'Craven A'. The different brand makes were given a value rating by us which would be agreed by all the other gangs in the surrounding area. The 'Woodbine Packet' would be valued at one pound, the 'Kerry Blue' - five pounds, 'Gold Flake' - twenty pounds, the 'Craven A' - fifty pounds, and the 'Capstan' was 'king' at a hundred pounds.

The boys and I used to check out hotels and banks for the rare and valuable 'Capstan' box. To find one or two was obviously time well spent. So fag boxes became a symbol of power and wealth - the more you had the 'richer' you were, when you appeared at the top of the lane with your stack of 'money' for a game of 'Pontoon' or 'Snap' you got measures of respect from your fellow card players and of course they would have their stack too. The 'money' would be neatly tied with an elastic band and laid out in front of each individual and if you were carrying 'a large pile' it was important to have 'an assistant' to ensure nobody pulled a fast one by trying to rob you.

Sisters, Pauline and Sheila standing outside the North Chapel.

The 'assistant' usually covered the bets for the dealer in the popular game of Pontoon. As there would be anything up to six playing at the one time the assistant kept the game flowing smoothly, at the end of the session he would get a percentage of the profits providing of course there was no 'Baa' during the game. The 'Baa' factor was an ever present threat constantly hovering over every game and always created an amount of nervous tension, especially when one or two of the lads got broke early in the game and shouted "all A Baa". Immediately all hell would break loose, every player would be involved. There would be a dive to grab as much 'money' as possible. Imagine the scene, the lads that got broke saw a chance of getting their own back with the others trying to protect their new found winnings. This would be a real free for all, have no doubt about it. This was street violence - digging, hair pulling, kicks, the lot, no Marquess of Queensbury Rules here. The 'Baa' would be over as soon as it started, peace would be restore. There would be name calling, bad language and insults traded. There would be one or two bloody noses or cut lips, but so what, things were back to normal, the law of the jungle prevailed. The card game would resume again with a solemn pledge that no further 'Baa' would take place during that particular session, anyway it was an unwritten rule that a second 'Baa' would never take place at the same card school.

The card game most likely to cause 'A Baa' was 'Snap', where the players couldn't see their cards until they put it face up on the other players card if one player turned a king and the next player also turned a king all hands would shout 'Snap!', each claiming the other shouted first so it is very easy to imagine the difficulties that could arise, so 'Snap' was played as a last resort. We nicknamed it 'kamikaze' because it was suicidal to play it. Sometimes 'foreign currency' would be introduced, the lads would go down the quays to the ships from foreign parts and ask crew members for fag boxes, bringing back 'Camel' and other exotic brands. Horse trading would take place to see how much would be bid for the foreign stuff which carried a greater value than native currency.

Flynny' was a great man to give the best price for the foreign stuff he was pretty wealthy because his father worked in a factory where there was a lot of people employed and they must have been all smokers. Flynny's old man collected all the empty boxes for him. You could do some serious trading with them, Anna used pay real money because she liked to give a supply to brother Larry.

I always made sure that Anna had enough to keep her going and if I was stuck for cash I could always do a deal with her. She always seemed to have a ready supply of money.

Coming up to bonfire night was a time of serious trading and hundreds' and 'thousands' would be exchanged for firewood for the various bonfires in the area. Guns, rifles, bows and arrows, catapults and all sorts of 'fudgies' could be traded for. American comics sent by relations in the U.S. were in big demand and fetched big prices at the regular 'auctions' held in Bulldog Lane. A Captain Marvel comic could cost a fortune, and so would a Tarzan, Superman, Wonder Woman, Batman and Robin.

One time we had to pay the Farren Street gang five thousand to release our member Phil Griffin after they captured her for a game of kiss and torture. We got our own back and more sometime later when we did a deal with them for the return of all their bonfire stuff, which we had taken in a raid on their secret 'hideout'.

Chapter 10

Just The Ticket

An other money making scheme was the annual Christmas draw for a certain harrier club. This club, like many others, depended on the Christmas Draw for its main source of funding for the year. The members of the Club were given an allocation of tickets which they distributed to family and friends, they expected all the tickets would be sold.

Each book consisted of twenty tickets at a cost of sixpence each the seller would return ten shillings for each book so for selling a book of tickets there was a profit, it was rather small and one would need to sell many books to make a decent profit. The tickets had many prizes so people buying the tickets felt they were in with a good chance. The first prize was usually twenty five pounds donated by a prominent politician whose name would appear on all the tickets (it was a way of cheap advertising with an election around the corner). The other prizes carried the name of the donor(s) more often than not it would be from business people in the area.

In November the tickets would become available, the lads and myself would approach the various members of the

Club. We would be given a certain amount from each, neither knowing that we were taking tickets from anybody else. We would end up with around forty books a man. That was a lot of selling, as the prizes were always good the tickets virtually sold themselves.

The selling began in earnest. As usual the territory was divided amongst the three of us we had been doing the selling for the past three years, we had regular customers. For about three weeks we were hard at it calling to every shop, pub, factory, office and house in our particular territory until every ticket was sold. In money terms we would have sold twenty pounds each, this was a fortune to have in sweaty little hands. Soon we would put our plan into action.

The 'plan' was that we would hold the money and the counterfoils of the tickets until a couple of days before the draw took place. The men who gave us the tickets would be getting worried at this stage, but they need not have feared, we would deliver, but only some. Each man who gave us ten books would get six books returned. All sorts of excuses were made by us, we were waiting for the person in the house, the pub, the shop to return the tickets sold or unsold. As the Sunday of the draw was approaching we knew the Club members were anxious to get tickets or counterfoils and money returned. The three of us would make two pounds each on the scam, not a bad profit at all we agreed.

We kept the counterfoils of tickets we had sold but hadn't returned to the club member. But our plan would ensure that every ticket we sold would be in that draw. We would never let a good customer down. On the Sunday Afternoon prior to the draw a crowd from the area would gather in the club, all the counterfoils would be scattered on a huge table and many hands would be busy removing the staples and folding the individual tickets, getting them ready for the drum from which they would be drawn later that night. At this point we would be 'as busy as bees' folding the tickets then, when we had a big bundle in front of us, we would slip the counterfoils which we had hidden up our sleeves on to the bundle before us, thus ensuring that all our customers got into the draw. This was a matter of honour.

When we successfully completed our mission, which ensured all our customers were in, it was home for tea and back that evening for the big draw. The Club would be packed with people for this annual event as they waited with excitement for the Draw to commence. One occasion I could not believe my ears as the first prize was called out. It was won by an aunt of a certain politician who was later to go on to become Taoiseach and my name was called out as the seller. Later I would receive my reward from the prizewinner but the most important thing was that I would be regarded as lucky and thus ensure increased sales the next time around.

A view of Blackpool in the 1940s.
(Courtesy Shay Curtin's Cork Heritage Collection)

Chapter 11

Denny's Cellar
- The Great Clean Up

The great thing about summer holidays from school was the thought of all the money we were going to make from Denny's cellar which was situated in Hodders Lane, off Gerald Griffin Street, and extended all the way to the Watercourse Road. It was a huge complex which employed hundreds of men and women, all from around the Northside. Denny's Meats and sausages were famous all over Ireland and abroad, but, for people who lived in the vicinity it was that smell they all remembered.

It was a horrible smell, no words could describe it and it seemed to be everywhere all the time. It was at its worst in hot weather. We could do nothing about that smell we just got used to it.

Dennys was a thriving business, every day hundreds of lorries of all shapes and sizes would be lined up in Gerald Griffin Street, stretching down as far as O'Connell Street, waiting to off load their cargo of animals. The squealing of the pigs intermingled with the bellowing of cattle and the baa-ing of sheep was an all too familiar everyday sound. This was a regular feature of daily life in our area that time and though a nuisance to the neighbours we got used to the sounds, just as we did the smells. The nuns in the convent were constantly complaining to the management and appeals to the Gardaí on the Watercourse Road was futile as they had to suffer the smell also.

Unlike some of our questionable moneymaking activities the money we made from Denny's Cellar was 'legit, real honest to God, hard earned.

As soon as a lorry drove in to off-load Bill, Pat and myself would pull a 'gantry' up to the back of the lorry. We would hunt the pigs or sheep or cattle from the lorry down the 'gantry' into the cellar yard where Tadhg Stout (from Denny's) would direct the animals into pens. Later, in the day Connie, who was built like Charles Atlas, would have the gorey job of slitting the throats of the hundreds of pigs. We didn't like to think of that part, although we often watched as Connie 'operated'.

Then, the real hard work for us would begin, cleaning out the lorries, now empty of their cargo would be full of straw and animal dung. Even though the 'pong' was unmerciful we got stuck into the cleaning with our brushes and a pike which we 'borrowed' from some pig farmer. When the lorry was cleaned the driver would give us sixpence (a tanner) each, which we considered good. Some times the Lorry owner would ask you to go to the shop, for Mick McQuaid plugged tobacco. He might tell you to 'keep the change' from the ten shilling note. God knows we were tempted to do a runner more than once with the beautiful crispy ten 'bob' note but agreed we would be only 'killing' ourselves if we did that.

Management and staff of Henry Denny and Sons, Watercourse
Road in the1930s.

Every morning of the summer holidays the three of us would
be down at the cellar around eight thirty in time for the first
lorry and to beat off rivals who would be trying to muscle in
on what we considered our territory. Though we were
considered a nuisance by Denny's, Tadhg turned a blind eye
to our activities, except when senior management were about
the place (Tadhg) would tell us to clear off out of here' but
when the coast was clear he always gave us a welcome back.
Apart from the money we earned cleaning out the lorrys
Dennys Bacon factory was a serious contributor to our
financial well being. On a regular basis we would go to the
cellar and collect meat and pickle for the many shops in the
area, every body had a family relative who worked in
Dennys. Mother worked there, as did her father.

Chapter 12

In Praise Of The Range And The Sawdust Fire

In the late forties and early fifties poverty and hard times was ever present throughout Ireland, and Cork, like the rest of the bigger cities had its share of such deprivation. Yet there was always a great spirit of co-operation between everybody. Gerald Griffin Street where I was born and bred, was renowned for its marvellous neighbours. We regarded ourselves as Blackpool people and were proud of it! Basic items like tea, sugar, bread, butter and cigarettes were always in short supply and ration books were issued to everybody.

Neighbours would constantly borrow butter, tea and sugar from each other, "Go next door and ask Nelly for a few spoons of tea until next week," Ma would order me, "and tell her I have a couple of spare Woodbines (cigarettes) for her if she wants them." That's the way it was with most people in the neighbourhood, constantly borrowing off each other to keep the family going, all mothers were miracle workers.

Amongst the many challenges of these days was the concern for heating the house in times when winters were harsher (and the summers long and beautiful). Fuel was always scarce, coal was too expensive and a luxury, turf was more plentiful and timber blocks when available were sold from door to door.

Firelighters were in great demand for starting the fire. A firelighter comprised a small bundle of wood tightly bound with binding twine and wooden shavings dipped in creosote. Again the order from Ma,
"Go up to Dinny Sullivans, for a peck of coal, and on your way back, call to O'Neills in Farren Street for two halfpenny firelighters."

Blocks of wood would also be in demand, if you had the money you could get a big bag from O'Shea's Timber Yard on the Watercourse Road. Then the mode for transporting the blocks from the Timber Yard to home was produced - the faithful boxcar (which during the week would double as a chariot or stagecoach when we were 'playin' cowboys and Indians). The boxcar was made of wood. It was, as the name implies, made like a box with two long handles one on either side which were called the 'shafts'. Underneath the box an axle with two ballbearing wheels which were well greased for speed. (Sometimes if there was no boxcar, the family pram would be utilised to do the necessary. No point in having it lying idle in the corner and the next baby not due for another six months!)

There was no electricity and gas was in short supply (and expensive). Many a time when mother ran short of money she would put a miraculous medal into the gas meter and it worked. See what I mean about the mothers being miracle workers. Then when the man from the gas company came round to collect the money from the gas meter he would give mother back the miraculous medals. She would be embarrassed and would say "those bloody kids were at it again". The neighbours were always excited when the gas man came round for it meant that they would get some few pennies back, but the gas man had to allow for the medals. We were lucky in our house because we had the range, the name we gave the large black cooker which had a prominent, and proud, position in our kitchen. The range was our only source of heating and cooking at that time and it had to be treated like a baby, as indeed it was!

My Nanny Allen would give me a three penny piece every Saturday for polishing and cleaning the range. She would supply me with a box of black lead (polish) and two brushes, one for putting on the blacklead and the other for polishing, as Nan said, "Until you can see your face in it", such was the reverence in which the range was held. During the course of cleaning I discovered where Nan kept her snuff in a 'secret' alcove in the range, it remained a secret with me. She would not want me to know she 'snuffed' but we all knew anyway.

If the 'range' was overburdened with too much demand we would bring out the Sawdust fire. What a faithful friend was the good old sawdust fire! Made from a five gallon oil drum it had the top cut off and a hole drilled in its bottom, it stood on two blocks of concrete in the backyard. It was packed tightly with sawdust from top to bottom. A hole was made right down through the sawdust with the handle of the sweeping brush. Two slender pieces of iron would be put along the top of the drum to rest the cooking pot on. You would then apply a match to the sawdust through the bottom hole, and slowly but surely the sawdust would take light, and burning slowly, would cook the meal or the brown bread in no time at all. The sawdust fire was a great friend in those days and as a kid I loved to pack in the sawdust and get the fire going.

Many years later every house in our area got the 'electric'.

Chapter 13

Nowhere The Also Ran Greyhound

We never knew where the greyhound came from so we called him 'Nowhere', which in hindsight was a spark of inspiration (it seemed so at the time).

A far as we were concerned 'Nowhere' just simply turned up on our doorstep one day and adopted us or even the other way round. Mother would have none of it and told us to "get rid of 'that dog', wasn't one enough sure hadn't we the poor old mongrel 'Browny' with the big sore on his back to take care of". What mother didn't know that one night we tried to drown 'Browny' because we thought he was in terrible pain from that sore on his back so we brought him down to the river by Camden Quay. We put a rope with a big stone tied to it round poor 'Browny's neck and threw him into the water. Then crying our eyes out the three of us ran into Saint Mary's Dominican Church to say a prayer for 'Browny's soul (and our own souls as well). We lit a candle each for him and promised St. Dominic we would come back later with the money for the candles. I don't think we ever did – (God, we must do that). The three of us cried all the way home conscience stricken for what we did to faithful Browny' though we thought it was the right thing at the time. We were wondering how we would explain to Mother. We need not have worried for when we arrived at our house we were amazed to see Browny sitting on the doorstep dripping wet with the rope still around his neck. The stone, thankfully, had fallen off as Browny hit the water.

The sight of 'Browny' turned our tears to joyous ones as we hugged and kissed him all over, not the least worried that we were also kissing that sore on his back. We dried him then we took him in home, ashamed now at our attempt to drown him. We vowed solemnly to God and Our Lady to love and cherish 'Browny' for as long as he lived. Now we had two dogs 'Browny, and 'Nowhere', the Greyhound.

We decided we would train the greyhound to race and convinced Mother that we would make loads of money with 'Nowhere'. We took advice from Flynny, who said he knew a thing or two about greyhounds and he did too because his sister was married to a farmer out in Waterfall who had greyhounds which Flynny fed and walked from time to time. He told us 'Nowhere' could turn out to be a 'flyer' but needed to be fed. "Meat and stout", he said "would be great". "Where in God's name", we chorused "will we get meat and stout from?"
"I'll tell ye", said Flynny, "if I can go halves in the dog I'll feed him and train him and we'll split the winnings fifty/fifty, down the middle when he wins races up in the Greyhound Track on the Western Road." We agreed with Flynny's plan and spat on each others palm to seal the deal.

Thanks to Flynny's expertise 'Nowhere' began to look better after a couple of weeks but Flynny said that he couldn't keep on taking the food and stout from his brother in laws dogs to feed our dog. We said we understood and discussed a game plan. Flynny said raw meat was most important for 'Nowhere'. We decided to do something about it as Coughlan's Butchers shop was just two doors away we decided to start there. The plan was simple, Pat would go in and divert Mr. Coughlan's attention by asking him did he want any 'pickle' from Denny's Cellar? While they were talking I would whip a couple of chops from the front window.

'Nowhere' was by now better fed than any of us and we continued to 'borrow' a regular supply of chops from Mr. Coughlan. We were 'haunted' he never found out or he would certainly have given us the 'chop'! Despite Flynny's best efforts he informed us that 'Nowhere' was not … well going nowhere or even anywhere.

A lost cause, "Jaysus" said Flynny "I can run faster myself". This news was devastating to the three of us. So what were we to do? We stopped taking Mr Coughlan's chops. Flynny relinquished his fifty per cent slice of the action. There was no where for 'Nowhere' to go. We thought about doing a 'Browny', but we remembered our promise to Holy God. Anyway, as luck would have it the problem solved itself. One day I was taking 'Nowhere' from our back yard for a walk, but before I could slip the lead on him he bounded away from me and ran up our stairs, he jumped through the open window, landed on the back yard wall and with one mighty leap he landed on Bulldog Lane and took off like an express train heading at a mighty sped toward the Watercourse Road. 'Nowhere' had at last shown potential. Was he trying to tell us something - we never found out.

* * *

Definitions

BAA	A sudden exclamation by a pitch and toss or card player which signals a rush by everybody to grab the stake.
Blocks	Going to Fetch Firewood (Blocks of)
Pickle	A mixture of water, pigs blood and salt in which meat was put in to keep it (the meat) fresh before refrigeration came in.
Lop(s)	A slang word for a penny coin.
Ten Bob	Slang for a half pound note (Irish)
Toblerone	Probably the longest bar of chocolate in ireland and still much in demand.
Lane(way)	Off-shoot roadway to main street
Flashing	Putting on display. To tease.
Hanky	Hankerchief.
Five Pound Note	Irish currency (about ten US dollars)
Flag (Days)	Miniature flags pinned to a collection box and bought for charities.
Checks	Slang for slot or gaming machines
Farthing	The smallest/least coin ever in Irish currency.
Back Yard	Piece of ground at rear of house
Range	A heating Stove upon which meals were cooked.
Sawdust Fire(s)	Five gallon oil drum packed with sawdust and then lit to cook food upon.
Garda (Downey)	Name for an Irish policeman (cop)
Fag Boxes	Empty cigarette packets used as a form of currency in the 30s, 40s & 50s by rival gangs for cardplaying, etc.
Draw	To draw/raffle ticket for prizes
Taoiseach	Prime Minister/President U.S.
Cellar (Denny's)	Abbotoir (Denny's Abbotoir)
Ration Books	A book(s) of stamps issued by the government for food allocation (war time food stamps)
Peck (of coal/turf)	A measure of fuel, i.e. coal
Box Car	A timber box with wheels and two shafts - handcraft.
Stout	Beer, Porter, Guinness Stout, Murphy's Stout, Beamish Stout.
Go Halves	Take a 50/50 stake/share.
Haunted	Very lucky (we were haunted)
Conjun Box	A metal box with an opening appeture used for saving money in.
Ten Pounds	Irish Currency pre decimal era

Following-up-one	Film serial or sequel.
Rasa	Raspberry Cordial, "A Glass of Rasa".
Donkey's Gudge	or chester cake made of different left over cakes and breads.
"Halfs"	Expression to share equally 50/50
The Lido	Name of popular cinema in Blackpool, Cork, Ireland.
Split	To be hit, injured, attacked.
Split	Slang for sharing - 50/50 split.
Julia Healy's Shop	Where milk and cakes were served, i.e. as in a soda fountain, USA.
Thompsons Doughnuts	Cream cakes made by Thompsons, Cork.
Wran	Following the Wren, an ancient irish custom when money is given to children as they go singing from house to house on St Stephen's Day, 26th December.
Bating	Meaning to beat at each door with a branch of holly.
Deck	Pack of playing cards, deck of cards.
Dogwide	Very much aware, clued in.
Shagging	A swear word common to the time.
A Blinder	Doing very well, winning much.
Scoop the School	Clean out the participating players of their money.
Pay	To call 17s, pay 17s as dealer in "21" Pontoon.
Three Pee	Three pennies, three dimes.
Tanner	Six pennies
Pitch and Toss	A game of heads and tails with coins played on street corners.
Fecking (school)	Title given to describe players of the game Pitch and Toss, a School/Location.
Fecker	A specially prepared piece of wood upon which two coins are placed for a game of Pitch and Toss prior to tossing coins into the air.
Harps (Tails)	as in heads and tails.
Heads	Heads (Common to all, heads or tails)
Flyers	A special pair of tossing coins (in the air) carried by individual tossers.
Tosser	Name given to Pitch and Toss players.
Ducking-in	Getting in by stealth without paying.
"Mon" Boy	Boy pupils of the North Monastery Christian Brothers School, Our Lady's Mount, Cork (Author educated there)

Chapter 14

A Play At Christmas

The period coming up to Christmas seemed the most challenging and encouraged us to strive to greater heights of invention in the pursuit of … let's be blunt - Money, Cash, Dosh, Moula … Call it what you will! Many ideas were discussed and rejected until finally it was decided - we would do a 'Nativity Play'. Billy, Pat and myself chose the 'Cast' very carefully. We decided to offer the best parts to those whose parents were well off. In other words 'The Cast' was chosen not for their talent but because they would sell the required amount of tickets and deliver a nice little profit for us. Our darling mother thought the idea was lovely and allowed us the use of the big spare room for the play. As producer it was my job to allocate the various parts. Tommy Kavanagh was 'Baby Jesus'. His cherubic face making him a certainty for the part. Kathleen Cummins was 'Mary' because her mother promised her that she could use her much cherished 'Child of Mary Robe'. Jim O'Sullivan would be a perfect St. Joseph and who better for the part of the Three Wise Men than Foley, Flynny and 'Blackie' White. John Long was made for the part of King Herod and Dan Coleman, Alec Morrissey and Bridie Morrissey (no relation to Alec) were given the part of Herod's soldiers. Brothers

Billy and Pat were appointed security ... just in case there would be a raid on the box office by the Farren Street Gang. The script took the form of a pep talk from me. How Jesus was born in a stable with the Three Wise Men following the star to Bethlehem. Then King Herod wanted to kill all the little babies and the play would end with Jesus, Mary and Joseph and the Flight into Egypt. Sure they all knew the story anyway and would be able to do this play off the top of their heads. They didn't need scripts or anything like that.

The news spread like wildfire 'The Nativity Play' was going to be on in our house and many a 'conjun' box was raided to buy a ticket. In no time the play was a sell out. The cast had delivered and in advance. I could never remember having ten pounds in my hands all at once. I opened an account in the Savings Bank beside Saint Mary's Hall Picture House. Mr. Corkery himself took the seven pounds from me (I kept three pounds back for 'expenses', milk and cakes for the cast).

The Show ran for ...er - The Nativity Play ran for three nights at half past six and the matinee was on Saturday at twelve noon it had to finish at two because the following-up-one was on in The Lido at three and we couldn't miss that.

During the run of the play Pat made a real 'killing' selling glasses of 'Rasa' and slices of 'Donkey's Gudge' which mother had made. Pat was disappointed when Billy insisted on "halfs". It was a tough old station, it was split or be split. The play went off without a hitch, well almost there was a few first night nerves, especially when 'Baby' Jesus stood up in the orange box ('Crib') shouting that he had to do his toilet just as the Three Wise Men were presenting their gifts. After that incident I warned Tommy not to drink Rasa before the show.

Snowball battle on the Mardyke. *Note bare footed boy third from left. (Courtesy Irish Examiner).*

The show was coming to a close, it was Saturday at noon. High noon as it turned out. As the play was coming to a close I was overcome with a desire to get up to Julia Healy's Shop as fast as I could for I had realised that Saturday was a busy day for Julia and she might run out of my favourite cakes. I slipped away unnoticed (or so I thought) and up the street into the oasis that was Julia Healy's Milk and Cake Shop on Shandon Street. As it turned out Julia was not that busy I got immediate attention from this small, stocky woman in her long, white coat and her shock of steel grey hair tied in a bun on the top of her head.

"A pint of milk, and three Thompsons doughnuts, please Mrs. Healy," said I, in a mannerly tone.
She had it ready in a flash and I settled into my favourite spot, The Nook, just inside the front door and the frosted glass offered great privacy, even secrecy. I was into my second pint of milk when there was a commotion at the

front door. I recognised the voices.

"Where is he?" said the voice of 'Blackie' White.

"Here he is behind here," said Dan Coleman.

Suddenly what seemed like twenty pairs of hands, grabbed me, turned me upside down on the street and just shook me 'till the money fell from my pockets. I couldn't catch my breath, I felt the milk and cakes coming up my throat. I pleaded with them to let me explain but the 'Cast' wouldn't hear of it, they felt betrayed, they were really angry. The Three Wise Kings turned my pockets inside out and took every penny from me. One of the soldiers, Alec Morrissey cried out in a loud voice, "Seize his legs and take off his shoes and socks!" "Oh My God!" I thought, "I'm really in for it now!" as Dan Coleman and Bridie Morrissey tore off the shoes and socks in record time and Bridie held aloft the prize ... the Bank Book with the seven pounds that I had lodged just the day before.

Bridie handed the book to King Herod who decreed that I be frog-marched over to the Savings Bank (they opened Saturdays) and withdraw the money which would be divided between the cast. 'Baldy' Corkery, the Bank Manager paid out the money ... All seven pounds, and warned me not to come near the bank again, wasting his time, lodging money on a Friday and drawing it out on Saturday was just not on. Now the cast had every penny of the box office take - they wouldn't give me the price of The Lido and Foley looked disdainfully at me and said,

"You're a lucky man the play was not 'The Stations of the Cross' we would have crucified you to Julia Healy's Door."

* * *

Chapter 15

St. Stephen's Night - Completely Sold Out

It was St. Stephen's night Father and Mother went off to visit their friends, Nell and Flor, I as the eldest was left in charge of 'The House'. This particular occasion we decided to invite some of our own friends in to play cards - Pontoon, it was, "The only game in town," we were going to play for money. Real money, it with our pockets full after being out on the 'Wran' (Wren) that day we were 'loaded' after 'bating' down every door in the neighbourhood and beyond. Foley, Flynny, 'Blackie' White, Coleman, John Long, Alec Morrissey all accepted the invitation and arrived to be greeted by Pat, Bill and myself.

We sat round the large table in the kitchen stripped of the Christmas tablecloth we were about to get down to business with me producing the deck of cards and shuffling the pack. When Flynny asked to see the 'Deck' as he wanted to count them. But he didn't count them. He examined them very carefully and as he scrutinised the back of each card I was getting a bit nervous, in fairness to Flynny he was 'dog wide'. He would look at the back of a card and say, "Betcha that's an 'Ace'." He would flip it over, yes it was an 'Ace'. He'd go on, "Betcha that's a shagging 'king'," and it was! Well the game was up before it even started. Flynny spotted our 'marked' deck if this had happened out in the street there would have been absolute murder but as it was in our house peace was restored after a barrage of language most foul and dire threats. Foley intervened to say that he had a brand new unopened deck that he got in his Christmas stocking. He ran down the street to his house in Hodders Lane and was back in no time with the brand new unopened, pack of cards. So in this uneasy atmosphere I was to deal first as it was my house, Bill and myself would "go in halves" which meant we would pool an equal amount of cash. I would be the dealer, Bill the cashier.

Pat decided he would not play cards, he had other plans for later. Before the card game commenced we all stood up touching each others hand we solemnly promised that there would be 'No Baa' in my house that night.

Bill and myself were playing a blinder. It was one of these inspired occasions when it seemed as if nothing could go wrong. I could twist on nineteen and get a deuce, if I had eighteen and four cards I would twist and get a two or a three and scoop the 'school' with a five card trick. There was one memorable tense and dramatic game which involved me and 'Blackie' White. There was at least two pounds in the pot which included a brand new crispy ten bob note belonging to 'Blackie', which he had taken from his account in the Penny Bank in Saint Mary's Hall. The tension was immense, the lads were after throwing in their hands and were watching the unfolding drama. You could hear a pin drop … 'Blackie' had four cards, he said he was 'stuck' which meant he was 'happy', as dealer I turned my two

cards over, I had a total of 'sixteen' and a dilemma. I felt as
Blackie had four cards he must have more than sixteen, what
was I to do? Under the circumstances any dealer worth his
salt would twist another card but as I pondered, looking
heavenwards for inspiration, from the corner of my eye I
could see Bill as he leaned back behind Blackie White, I saw
Bills lips move as he mimed the word 'Pay' at me. The mime
of Bills with the word 'Pay' suggested to me that despite
having four cards Blackie had only a total of sixteen as I had
sixteen with two cards if I said "Pay Seventeen's" I was the
winner. Normally, any dealer would twist another card but I
got the message from Bill amidst incredible tension I
declared in a loud voice "Pay Seventeen's," Blackie White
threw down his cards in disgust and disbelieve at 'my
cowardice' as Bill and I were about to scoop the pot of cash
all hell broke loose. Blackie suspecting some sort of
collusion or trickery, could take no more and despite
agreement to the contrary Blackie unleashed the dreaded
"Baa" word. In a flash everybody jumped for the money on
the table a free-for-all ensued with fists flying everywhere
and money and cards flying all over the place. Peace was
restored eventually, brokered by Pat who suggested a
compromise, Blackie would be given back his stake (which
included the now crumpled ten bob note).

With harmony restored things settled down and play
continued. Pat came into his own when he announced that
"Food and Drink was now being served" at a price "three
pee" for a slice of turkey, "two pee" for a slice of spiced
beef, tuppence halfpenny for a glass of "Rasa" and a slice of
"Christmas Cake, Madeira or Currant" and "last but by no
means least," Pat declared, "a thick slice of Christmas
Pudding with a dollop of custard, a tanner."

The money flowed freely. The lads were voracious, they

couldn't get enough. Soon Pat declared he was "sold out" and how he cleaned up, but there would be hell to pay when Mother and Father returned home and found all the food gone? Well Pat thought of that too and when the lads went home around 10 o'clock he counted all the money and as a form of compensation for Mother he got two clothes pegs and attached a pound and a ten shilling note to them hung them on the clothes line in the kitchen with the following note attached,

"For our Dear Mam,
Thanks for everything, and we mean everything!
All our love - The Boys."

Then we cleaned the mess from the various excesses and were just in bed when we heard our parents returning. We distinctly heard mother exclaim in delight when she saw the money pegged to the clothes line. She bounded up the stairs to thank her little darlings but we dreaded the morning when she would look in the cupboard and, like old Mother Hubbard …..

Gerald Griffin Street in later years. (Cooke's Cork Collection)

Chapter 16

Pitch And Toss School
A Real Education

An easy way to spend hard earned money was playing Pitch and Toss or 'Feck' as it was more commonly known. 'Fecking Schools' were held in many working class (or at the time workless class) areas of the city North and South. Our favourite 'School' was held in The Quarry, in Johnson's Lane just off Gerald Griffin Street. Tossing was in itself an art form and every tosser had his own special pair of halfpennys which were called 'Flyers' they were always kept bright and shiny. Most tossers would have a 'Fecker' a piece of wood about three or four inches long upon which the flyers were placed. The Fecker was cleaned with sandpaper to keep it smooth and clean. The Tosser would religiously place his beloved 'Flyers' on his trusty 'Fecker' and then, demanding attention and adequate room to toss, he would assume a pose as he was about to hurtle the halfpennys skyward. Every individual had his own style. Some would go down on one knee - then deftly thrust the flyers toward the heavens and as they took flight the tosser would invoke the great God of Feck to return his flyers to earth with the two shiny heads looking upward indicating that the tosser had won the bets on the ground.

Should the Gods be angry and return 'Harps', then the tosser would call on Beelzebub and other devils to hurtle the fecking god to Hades.

A wonderful and thrilling game at which fortunes were won and lost it was not for the faint hearted as many a participant will recall you would literally be taking your life in your hands if you decided to attend what was euphemistically called a 'fecking school'. One would have to be constantly

Lane off Paul Street with Shandon Steeple in background.
(Courtesy Irish Examiner)

on the alert for trouble, particularly if one or two of the Boys were losing too much of their money or even, worse again, if they had lost it all. They would wait their opportunity for a big sum of money to be on the ground, then as the attention of everybody was on the 'flyers' winging their way upwards the Boys would yell out the apoplectic words, "What did the sheep on the mountain say" - "All a Baa" it was akin to a war cry as everybody dived to the ground to grab whatever money they could. Boots, fists, entire bodies would be flying everywhere, then it would be over in a few seconds despite bloody noses, cut lips, split heads, sore had etc. No matter, the game would resume as if nothing happened, the money and the bets once more on the ground, 'flyers' spinning and spiralling rocket-like from the fecker to fall to earth in seconds heralding the destiny of the hard earned few pennies on the ground.

Though Pitch and Toss was great fun it had its dark side with its fair share of dodgy characters who would attempt to introduce double headed halfpennys to ensure that they would win everytime. One occasion Pat and myself were at a game in The Quarry, where we were victims of the 'double headers'. I lost my money and Pat's money also he threatened to tell mother which panicked me somewhat so I was left with no alternative but to call a "Baa" I dived in, grabbed some money and Pat and I then ran like hell, pursued by showers of stones and pieces of slate which could have inflicted serious damage. I was hit on the head by a piece of slate which drew considerable blood but I didn't mind, I would have been more worried about what mother would do to me after losing Pat's money. 'Fecking Schools' alas are no more but fond memories linger on of the places we played, Johnsons Lane, the Butter Market, Quarry Lane, The 'Lido Lane', Dublin Hill to mention afew.

Chapter 17

The Lido For Excitement

W hat a great choice of picture houses we had in those days. There were eleven in all, The Savoy in Patrick Street, The Pavilion also in Patrick Street, The Palace and Coliseum in MacCurtain Street, The Ritz in Washington Street, The Lee in Winthrop Street, The Assembly Rooms (better known to us as 'The Ass & Belly') in the South Mall, The Capitol on the Grand Parade, The Imperial or Miaha's in Oliver Plunkett Street, but our favourites were in the Northside, St. Mary's Hall opposite the North Cathedral and the all time favourite, The Lido in Blackpool where love stories began and ended all in the same night. Better known as 'The Ranch' it was our 'dream palace' we loved it and lived for the 'following up' ones like Captain Marvel, Flash Gordon, Superman, The Lone Ranger, Johnny MacBrown, Gene Autrey The Singing Cowboy, Roy Rodgers and his horse 'Trigger', and sidekick Gabby Hayes and Batman and Robin, John Wayne was another great hero. God, we loved everything about The Lido and we would do anything, well almost anything, to make sure we had money for at least one or two visits every week. We wanted The Lido to go on for ever!

To generations of Corkonians, particularly from the Northside, The Lido Cinema holds very special memories.

'The Ranch' still stands on the Watercourse Road like a monument to a bygone era of cinematic enjoyment. To anyone who knew The Lido years ago, it is instantly recognisable today. Structurally nothing has changed from the outside. What was it like inside? Let's find out by stepping back in time, to the 1950s when the 'new look' in ladies fashions was just in vogue.

The cinema was divided in two tiers, the 'four penny hop' and the 'eight penny hop' on Sunday nights the price jumped to an enormous ten pence. The box office was on the left hand side as one went up the steps of the main entrance. You paid your four pence and got your ticket which was then torn in half by either 'Florry' or Tom (who looked the dead spit of Errol Flynn). Then 'ushered' to your hard bottomed seat in the front part, you fully intended to 'duck' back to the soft seats in the 'eight penny hop', that is if Mr. Coughlan or 'The Shadow' as the Manager was called, didn't emerge from the shadows and nab you.

The punishment was immediate and swift - OUT - and you didn't get your money back. Ducking into the soft seats was a military operation with split second timing and full of danger.

Ducking in for half price on Sunday nights was a real thrill enjoyed by the few who had the right connections. How well this scam was organised with at least two men involved. One would be inside the other outside on the street taking the money.

You would pay him two pence. He would give a knock, the door was be opened by his colleague inside and you would be told to 'keep the head down and move fast.' You were in for just half the price. It took the management a while to

The Lido Cinema in Watercourse Road in Blackpool, Cork, opened on 25th October 1931, (formerly the Blackpool Cinema). The Lido closed on April 14th 1962. It re-opened as the Palladium Cinema and closed in 1965. *Pic. courtesy: The Irish Examiner* cop on to this one. However on with the show. Lights down, then the whistling would start from the audience as the 'Ads' appeared, and the one that would get the greatest reaction was that offering £5 reward to anyone giving information about letting off fireworks or 'squibs' in the cinema. Well that ad was the proverbial red rag to a bull and the response was immediate. To a man (and indeed to a woman) a 'shower' of half-eaten apples or 'stucks' hit the screen with a vengeance, followed swiftly by a hail of cigarette butts, mainly Woodbines (and some Kerry Blues and Players Weights from well heeled owners). Needless to say that £5 was never claimed. Nobody wanted to die young. Despite the best efforts of the ushers with their flashlamps no culprits were apprehended and an uneasy peace would prevail, that is until the sing-a-long and the words of the song would come up on the screen and the soundtrack of 'darkies' singing 'Katie, Beautiful Katie', 'Old Man River' and a few more songs like that. This would arouse the sheer talent of the audience, each trying to out-do the other in howling like dogs.

In fairness to The Lido management they did try to introduce a bit of class now and then but to no avail. Like the time they introduced the girl with the sweet tray strapped around her neck and the flashlamp to show you where your favourite sweets and chocolates were. This innovation got a very quick death. The poor girl survived but she could never have been the same after. The things that happened to that poor girl. You would point to a bag of sweets with your right hand. The girl would flash her light towards that area and your left hand would be working overtime knocking off goodies in the unlit area of the tray.

This attempt at trying to 'Savoy' The Lido came to a bitter end when after a poor film someone shouted from the audience, "What did the sheep on the mountain say?" Now the only answer to that question is an almighty chorus of "Baa". As one the audience rose from their seats and dived in the direction of the poor girl, her tray of goodies was scattered all over the floor of the cinema after that it was every man and woman for themselves.

When 'normality' was finally restored the audience settled down, the main feature was followed by what we were here for anyway, "the following-up-one", Superman with Clark Kent and Lois Lane who both worked for The Planet news-paper. We were waiting with dry mouths to see would Superman save Lois Lane as she was falling from the 75th floor of the Empire State Building. Of course he would. There's a new following-up-one starting next week. They're just showing the trailer, Buster Crabbe as 'Flash Gordon', should be great. Can't wait to see this one, all about space and rockets and distant planets and "stuff like that".

Then the lights came on. It was all over for another night. The doors were flung open and released the hordes of 'Cowboys and Indians'. On imaginary horses we galloped and 'shot' our way home wondering how in God's name would we find the money to get into The Lido the next time?

* * *

Author's mother, Pricilla with her daughters Pauline and
Sheila on the strand in Youghal, August 1950

Chapter 18

Mother, The Greatest Cook Of All Time!

Christmas time in our house, was always a happy occasion and full of fond memories of delicious smells. Thanks to mothers marvellous cooking of a myriad of cakes which were always in constant demand. We scoffed them the instant they were taken from the oven. The family favourite was 'Donkey's Gudge', called Chester Cake by more gentile souls. 'Donkey's Gudge' was made from all sorts of leftovers, 'Heels' of bread, left over cakes, etc. plus some delicious spice flavouring which was part of mothers repertoire of secret recipes. From time to time we would help her to mix the ingredients in a large bowl and often would get a slap as we spooned the mix into our mouths if we thought she wasn't looking, mother seemed to have eyes in the back of her head. When the mix was ready it was poured into the cake tin or 'shape' then into the oven to bake. The aroma that wafted through our kitchen was comparable only to that from Curran's Bakery in the North Main Street. How often would Northsiders stop outside Curran's Bakery to savour that wonderful aroma.

Mother's cakes were the tops, the Queen Cakes with

sultanas (or raisins) arrayed like soldiers in their white paper cups will never be forgotten and her 'melt in the mouth' Apple Tart, especially with cloves added. Little wonder our house was always full with neighbours and friends. Mothers friends would bring the ingredients and she would do the baking. Christmas time was especially busy and in the weeks leading up to it she would be gathering ingredients bit by bit, Peal, essence of this and that, raisins and sultanas (how often did we eat them before they ever got near a cake) and then there was the Christmas Pudding that was to take pride of place on the Christmas table (next to the turkey - if we had one). How lovingly that Pudding was treated. The ingredients were mixed weeks in advance and allowed to mature, then it was time to boil it, a big cloth was produced, the mix was poured into the cloth which was tightly bound at the top and then placed in a huge pot to boil for hours and hours. Oh, the smell of that pudding as it boiled, when it was finally 'done' it was taken out and placed in a large bowl

The Magnier Family. Pictured back (l/r) Pat, Pauline, Shelia, Noel with Father and Mother John and Priscilla. *Insert: brother Bill.*

where it stayed until Christmas Day. On St. Stephen's Day mother, if we were good boys and girls, would fry some of the pudding on the pan which was something completely out of this world. Still it was the 'Donkey's Gudge' that remained our all-time favourite. It became a part of our staple diet an 'all year rounder'. It was to receive fame far beyond the boundaries of our house, legions of 'Mon' boys enjoyed some when we swapped for apples and pears. We traded slices with the local lads for American comics. When Billy Neville came home to Bulldog Lane on holidays from Fords Factory in Dagenham. He always brought back a 'slab' of 'Donkey's Gudge' to England when Uncle Tom came from America he also took some back with him to New York along with the recipe.

Whenever the supply of 'Donkeys Gudge' dried up the two boys and I would stand before Mother and recite a verse of our self-penned Mantra, "We bear no grudge against your 'Gudge'." Mother would scatter us out of the kitchen saying she's fed up cooking and baking for us, but not long after a delicious aroma would once again waft through our house and as we waited for the oven to open we would give Mother a lusty second verse of "We bear no grudge" ... to the air of a much revered hymn of the time. ... "Holy God We Praise Thy Name".

Author's Grandparents John 'Holly' Magnier and his wife Nora, Fermoy, County Cork.

Chapter 19

My Mother Priscilla
(1915-1989)

I would like to pay tribute to mothers everywhere in the world. In particular mothers from the era of the 1930s, 40s and 50s. They were the real heroes, repeating the miracle of the loaves and fishes on a daily basis and still finding time to laugh and sing. OK, so we had little of worldly possessions but really we did not know the difference, we were happy, mother saw to that. My mother, an only child coped well rearing three rascal sons during the war years, especially with father away in foreign parts with the British Army. As I recall it, we were always laughing and getting up to all sorts of "Devilment". That mother reigned supreme was fine by us. We loved Prissie with all our heart and soul. We love her still and forever.

Priscilla Magnier.

Priscilla was an avid reader and I can recall her swapping "The Oracle" and "The Miracle" magazines with her great lifelong pals Kate McCormack, Nell Maloney and May Linehan. I remember the three of them in my house talking in hushed tones as they flicked through the pages of a book called, "No Orchids For Miss Blandish". I never knew if this book was risqué or not to this day. Later on mother took up writing and composing songs (she had learned to play piano from a Mr. Siev a music teacher). She had a great love of poetry and taught us all "O My Dark Rosaleen".

As a tribute to mother I include her prose and poem on Murphy's Shaft written literally as she watched it being demolished and also her poignant poem of her beloved son Billy who was tragically lost at sea from the M.V. Irish Plane off the Florida Coast on the 7th May 1964.

Murphy's Brewery Shaft - God's Chimney

The first time I saw "Murphy's Shaft" (1856 to 1985) was from my pram. When we started Infant School, we used to say it was God's Chimney. When there wasn't any smoke coming from it we said, "Poor God will get cold". But Johnny, a little curly-haired kid told us not to be so silly because God could lift a finger and light it if he wanted to. So, that settled God's problem, and we were happy for Him.

When Johnny made his First Communion he was king or the lane for that day, and told us that his dad had climbed the "Shaft". We believed him and gave him all due respect for a while.

Now in October, nearly seventy years later, I watch "Murphy's Shaft" being hacked to bits. I see it from my back yard, being wiped from the skyline. Even as I write this, I feel the tears, not only in my eyes, but in my heart. Memories of "Bull-dog" Lane (so called because a man named Drummond lived there), of all my little friends, my Mam and Dad, and "Maggie" my beloved Gran. I suppose the lovely memories, like the Divine Assistance, will always remain with us, but even as I write this "they all come tumbling down".

So farewell, "Murphy's Shaft" you are wrapped in history. Our memories go with you like Autumn leaves.

Salute To The "Shaft"

Tall and straight and proud it stood
Watching over our childhood.
Red-bricked beauty, fore and aft
Our Guardian Angel, Murphy's Shaft!

It saw our laughter
Saw our tears, thro happy,
Sad and troubled years.
The sound of rifle-shot and shell
The toll of the Cathedral Bell.

It heard the Lee lap sweet and soft
And Father O'Flynn as he taught in the "Loft"
So Sláinte Shaft!
Your time has come,
But you shall not go un-sung
Now is the hour to toll the ·Bell
Alas! Poor Cork, I knew thee well.

Words and Poem by Priscilla Magnier

The Magnier family early 1950s
L-R: Pauline, Uncle Tom (Magnier,
USA), Priscilla (mother). Sheila.
Back L-R: Noel, John (Father), Bill.
Front: Pat with family pet dog "Pal".

My Great
Grandfather
David Kennedy

Only the railings of the North Cathedral, and the name J.J. Walsh still remain from this pre-war scene. Bailey's Lane was widened, to become Cathedral Road and St. Mary's Hall, to the right, was demolished. The Hall once housed a cinema and a 'Penny Bank'.